On Kwanzaa

written by **Judy Zocchi**
illustrated by **Rebecca Wallis**

3 1262 00014319 7

dingles&company New Jersey

©2006 by Judith Mazzeo Zocchi

All rights reserved. No part of this book may be reproduced in any form without written permission from the publishers, except by a reviewer who may quote brief passages in a review to be printed in a newspaper or magazine.

First printing

PUBLISHED BY dingles&company
P.O. Box 508 • Sea Girt, New Jersey • 08750
WEBSITE: www.dingles.com • E-MAIL: info@dingles.com

Library of Congress Catalog Card No.: 2004091572
ISBN: 1-891997-49-1

Printed in the United States of America

For Hazel Wilkins

ART DIRECTION & DESIGN Barbie Lambert
EDITED BY Andrea Curley
RESEARCH AND ADDITIONAL COPY WRITTEN BY Robert Neal Kanner
EDUCATIONAL CONSULTANT Anita Tarquinio-Marcocci
CRAFT CREATED BY the Aldorasi family
PHOTOGRAPHY BY Sara Sagliano
PRE-PRESS BY Pixel Graphics

Holiday Happenings examines the most popular holidays celebrated by various cultures. The series explains the origin of each day as well as popular traditions and activities associated with it.

Seven candles are placed in a candleholder (called a "kinara" in Swahili) that represents all African ancestors: a black one for the African people, three red ones for their struggles, and three green ones to symbolize hope for a better life.

On Kwanzaa
you bring out colored candles

Each day of Kwanzaa is dedicated to one of the seven principles: unity of family, self-determination, collective responsibility, cooperative economics, purpose, creativity, and faith. In the evening a family member lights a candle and explains which principle is being remembered on that day.

to light each night for a week.

Then you dress in African clothing to celebrate being unique.

> Many families decorate their homes with symbols of Kwanzaa. A straw mat ("mkeka") is placed on a table as a reminder of African traditions. Fruits and vegetables ("mazao") represent the harvest, and corn ("muhindi") symbolizes the children and the future hopes of the family.

On Kwanzaa
you put fruit and vegetables out on a mat

A special cup (a unity cup, or "kikombe cha umoja") is placed on the mat and filled with water, juice, or wine. A small amount is poured out to honor the ancestors and then the cup is passed around. Everyone sips from it to reinforce family unity.

and drink from a cup made of wood.

Then you learn about working together the way that you should.

On Kwanzaa
you could go shopping

One of the Kwanzaa principles is "cooperative economics" ("ujamaa"). This calls for African Americans to own their own businesses so that their communities can profit from them together.

> As a commitment to African history and tradition, many parents give their children symbolic gifts ("zawadi"). Typical gifts include books about Africa, tickets to African cultural events, and handmade clothing, art, and jewelry.

for gifts to give.

Then you **listen to stories** of how your ancestors lived.

> On the sixth night of Kwanzaa a great feast ("karamu") is usually held at a community center or church decorated with traditional African objects and the colors of Kwanzaa. During the feast, there are often ceremonies honoring ancestors and entertainment that includes African storytelling, music, and dancing.

On Kwanzaa
you might go to a feast

People who attend the feast usually bring traditional African food, including chicken casseroles, fried okra, black-eyed peas, corn fritters, and yams. The food is set on a large table in the center of the room.

and bring special foods to share.

Then you light the last candle as everyone says a prayer.

Harambee!

Kwanzaa is a seven-day African American cultural holiday that begins on December 26 and continues until January 1. It celebrates traditional African values of family, self-improvement, and community responsibility. Kwanzaa was created in 1966 by Dr. Maulana Karenga, a professor of black studies at California State University at Long Beach. He wanted to create a holiday that would bring African Americans together in celebration of their ancestry and culture. He created seven guiding principles for the holiday. He modeled them after ancient African harvest festivals, when communities came together to celebrate their crops, thank their creator, remember their ancestors, and share in the promise of the new year. Each day of Kwanzaa is celebrated with a candle-lighting ceremony dedicated to one of the seven principles: unity, self-determination, shared responsibility, cooperative economics, purpose, creativity, and faith. The name "Kwanzaa" comes from the Swahili phrase "matunda ya kwanza," which means "first fruits" in Swahili, the most widely spoken African language.

DID YOU KNOW...

Use the Holiday Happenings series to expose children to the world around them.

- During Kwanzaa, greetings and prayers are in Swahili, as it is the most widely spoken language of Africa. More than 50 million people speak Swahili.
- It has been reported that more than 18 million people worldwide observe Kwanzaa.
- Dr. Maulana Karenga, the founder of Kwanzaa, added a second "a" at the end of the Swahili word "Kwanza," which means "first fruits." He wanted the name of the holiday to reflect a difference between the Swahili word upon which it is based.
- The holiday colors of Kwanzaa–black, red, and green–go back to the ancient African Zinj Empires. Black represents the black people, red symbolizes the blood that was shed for the land they lost, and green stands for hope and Africa.

BUILDING CHARACTER...

Use the Holiday Happenings series to help instill positive character traits in your children.
This Kwanzaa emphasize attentiveness.

- Are you aware of your family heritage?
- Have you ever paid attention to the community in which you live?
- Do you notice how you fit into your family and community?
- How can you be more attentive and aware of your family and community?

CULTURE CONNECTION...

Use the Holiday Happenings series to expand children's view of other cultures.

- Find out which countries celebrate Kwanzaa.
- How do people in other countries celebrate Kwanzaa?
- Are these celebrations similar to the way people celebrate Kwanzaa in your country?

TRY SOMETHING NEW...
Spend time with one of your older relatives and ask him or her to tell you stories about your family's history. Then write a journal recounting the memories and facts that your relative shared with you. Type or write it out neatly and put it in a safe place so you will always have it as part of your family history.

For more information on the Holiday Happenings series or to find activities that coordinate with it, explore our website at **www.dingles.com**.

Craft Family Tree

Goal: To record your family's heritage

Craft: A family tree made from construction paper

Materials: Construction paper (brown, green, and another color of your choice), markers, scissors, and glue

Directions:

1. Make a list of your family members: grandparents, parents, siblings, and yourself. Count the number of people. (That's the number of leaves you will need to make.)

2. Using green construction paper, draw a leaf big enough to write a person's name on it. Make one for each person in your family. If you have several family members, you can put more than one name on a leaf.

3. Cut out the leaves using your scissors. Write the name of one family member on each leaf with a marker. Put the leaves aside.

4. Draw a tree trunk on a piece of brown construction paper. Then draw three large branches extending from each side of the trunk. You will have six branches total. Draw two little branches at the end of each large branch. Each of the three large branches stands for one generation of your family. Then cut it out.

5. Glue the tree trunk onto a sheet of construction paper. Take the leaves with your name and the names of your siblings and glue them to the ends of the large branches on the top level of your family tree.

6. Next, glue the leaf with your mother's name on it on the left-side branch of the middle level. Then glue the leaf with your father's name on it on the right-side branch of the middle level.

7. Finally, glue the leaves with the names of your mother's parents (your maternal grandparents) on the bottom branch under your mother's leaf. Then glue the leaves with the names of your father's parents (your paternal grandparents) on the bottom branch under your father's leaf.

8. You now have a three-generation family tree!

Judy Zocchi

is the author of the Global Adventures, Holiday Happenings, Click & Squeak's Computer Basics, and Paulie and Sasha series. She is a writer and lyricist who holds a bachelor's degree in fine arts/theater from Mount Saint Mary's College and a master's degree in educational theater from New York University. She lives in Manasquan, New Jersey, with her husband, David.

Rebecca Wallis

was born in Cornwall, England, and has a bachelor's degree in illustration from Falmouth College of Arts. She has illustrated a wide variety of books for children, and she divides her time between Cornwall and London.